Ketogenic Diet for Beginners

A Complete Guide with the Best Tips, Tricks, and Recipes for Weight Loss!

inattention, use or misuse of the information in question by the reader will render any resulting actions solely under their purview. There are no scenarios in which the publisher or the original author of this work can be in any fashion deemed liable for any hardship or damages that may befall them after undertaking information described herein.

Additionally, the information found on the following pages is intended for informational purposes only and should thus be considered, universal. As befitting its nature, the information presented is without assurance regarding its continued validity or interim quality. Trademarks that mentioned are done without written consent and can in no way be considered an endorsement from the trademark holder.

Table of Contents

Introduction

Congratulations on purchasing your personal copy of *Ketogenic Diet for Beginners.* Thank you so much for doing so! If you have come across this book because you wanted a guide that will lead you to the path of a healthier you, then you are in just the right place!

The following chapters will discuss some of the many reasons why you should make the choice to feel better about yourself, both inside and out, *today*, through the means of this successful diet!

You will discover how important it is to balance out your carb intake so that your body will have more room for food that is higher in fat that our bodies can use as a better source of fuel. If you have not been previously privy to what the ketogenic diet has to offer, you are in for a real treat! This diet is not a fad or a trend; it is one of the most utilized diets on the market! Your success solely depends on your willpower to steer clear of food that doesn't provide your body with the proper fuel to be the best you can be.

Within this book lie the basics of the ketogenic diet so you can wrap your mind around the grand concepts. Not sure where to start? No worries! This book is packed with a plethora of recipes to get you started on the right foot!

There are plenty of books about the ketogenic diet on the market, thanks again for choosing this one! Every effort was made to ensure it is full of as much useful information as possible. What are you waiting for? Dive in and start the process of becoming a healthier version of yourself! Good luck!

Introduction to the Ketogenic Diet

If you have purchased this book with not one clue as to what the ketogenic diet is, do not fret! This chapter will discuss and go into some detail about the most crucial aspects as to what makes this diet so successful!

The phrase 'ketogenic' is stemmed from the natural process of 'ketosis', which allows our bodies to thrive when the intake of food might be low. Ketones are produced during this process as fats break down in our livers. The entire goal of the ketogenic diet is to force our bodies to stay within this state of high metabolism. No, it is not about starving yourself and keeping yourself from consuming food, but rather the starvation of consuming carbohydrates. Humans have not changed in the fact that we can adapt to our environments at drastic speeds. That being said, when you pack your body with bad edibles, it will start to burn those precious ketones that are partially responsible for weight loss and optimum mental and physical performance.

Weirdly enough, the ketogenic diet has been around for quite a few decades. It was developed by a guy named Dr. Russell Wilder back in the year 1924. It was quite the concoction that treated epilepsy but unfortunately fell through due to the creation of anti-seizure medications that came about during the 1940's. It didn't make much of an appearance until the mid-1990's, when the Abraham family began the Charlie Foundation for their son, Charlie. Charlie's body did not handle all of that anti-seizure pill-popping very well. He began following the means of the ketogenic diet as a toddler and stuck to it for a time period of five years. He is now a successful college student and is still to this day seizure-free.

The bottom line is that the ketogenic diet is made up of extremely low-carb and high-fat intakes. This diet is quite similar to that of the Atkins and other low-carb diets. While you are reducing your intake of carbohydrates by such drastic amounts, you are replacing it with foods high in fat. The absence of carbs creates a highly metabolic state within your body, known as ketosis (as mentioned above.) In layman's terms, our body becomes an incredibly powered working machine, burning off fat for energy instead of ketones. It warps our metabolisms so that it no longer burns precious substances utilized to keep our bodies in the best shape they can be. This diet has been shown to reduce blood sugars and insulin levels, which makes it a diet that is loaded with quite a few health benefits. You will read about some of these benefits later in this chapter.

Different Types of Ketogenic Diets

- **High-protein ketogenic diet** – This form of the keto-diet is the same, but involves consuming more protein. The ratio required to stick to this diet is 60% fat, 35% protein and 5% carbohydrates.

- **Targeted ketogenic diet (TKD)** – This diet allows wiggle room to consume a bit more carbs as long as they revolve around workouts.

- **Cyclical ketogenic diet (CKD)** – This form of the keto-diet requires periods of high-carb intakes, such as 5 ketogenic days followed by a couple of high-carb intake days.

- **Standard ketogenic diet (SKD)** – This diet is the most utilized and recommended and requires one to consume moderate amounts of protein and high-fat. Usually involves 75% fat, 20% protein and 5% carbs.

The standard ketogenic version of the diet is the most sought out and recommended, as well as the most researched. The others are usually utilized by advanced individuals, such as athletes and bodybuilders.

Benefits and Risks of the Ketogenic Diet

All types of low-carb diets have been on the table of controversy for quite a few years. It has been said that diets high in fat content would raise cholesterol levels through the roof, causing heart disease and other bad body ailments. But research has been changing the face of low-carb dieting. It has been shown that amongst other diets, low-carb ones are the ones that seem to win the race. They are not only a great substitute when trying to lose weight, but they even have other great health benefits, even reducing cholesterol levels. Here are some ways that the ketogenic diet could produce some good things in your life!

Benefits

- The main component that is largely working in your body during your time on the ketogenic diet is the process of ketosis. Creating this metabolic state has been proven to have drastically positive effects, even if only on the diet for a short time. Here are some grand benefits of ketosis itself first!

  - Increases our body's capabilities to use fats as a source of fuel.

  - Ketosis has a protein-sparing effect, which means our bodies prefer utilizing ketones as opposed to glucose.

o   Lowers levels of insulin within our bodies, which contains a lipolysis-blocking effect, which reduces the utilization of fatty acids as a source of energy. When insulin levels are lowered, growth hormones and other growth factors can then be released without an issue.

- **Suppresses hunger** – Naturally, many diets require you to eat less than your body is used to. Because of this, never-ending hunger pains always seem to strike and at the worst times. This is the main reason people tend to feel miserable while on any diet plan. Diets that are low in carb intake are great because it automatically reduces your appetite. Those who cut carbs and consume more proteins and fat actually eat *fewer* calories.

- **More potential for weight loss** – It doesn't take a scientist to know that reducing the number of carbs we consume will directly contribute to weight loss. People who stick within the means of low-carb diets lose weight at a much faster rate. Diets low in carbohydrates tend to help in the reduction of excess water in our bodies, which can add on the pounds. The ketogenic diet reduces insulin levels too, meaning the kidneys are shedding all that excess sodium that can lead to retaining extra weight.

- **Reduction of triglycerides** – That long term is a fancy name for fat molecules. These little boogers contribute to ailments such as heart disease. When people reduce the consumption of carbs, there is quite a lessening of triglycerides building up in our bodies.

- **An increase of good cholesterol levels** – (HDL) is the kind of cholesterol you *want* to have. The ketogenic diet helps with raising the levels of HDL because of the consumption of fats. There are major bodily improvements when the levels of good and bad cholesterol start to shift.

- **Reduces blood sugar and insulin levels** – When we consume carbs, they are broken into simple sugars by our digestive system. They then go into our bloodstreams and elevate blood sugar levels. High sugars can be toxic, which is why insulin exists. There are many people who have a type of diabetes not only because of bloodlines and genetics, but because they have not eaten the best for quite a bit of their life. Their bodies no longer recognize insulin when it is attempting to help lower blood sugar levels. With the ketogenic diet, it has been seen that blood sugar and insulin levels come way down.

- **Reduction in blood pressure** – Diets that are low in carbohydrates are effective in reducing blood pressure levels, which can assist us in living longer. When blood pressure is high, we are at greater risks of developing hypertension and other ailments.

- **Natural treatment for cancer** – Properly regulating your body's metabolic functions has been proven to be a great step in reducing and even treating cancer. Reducing or totally removing carbs from your diet can help in the deletion of energy from cancerous cells and stop them from spreading.

- **Effective in treating metabolic syndrome** – This syndrome is a serious medical condition that is associated with heart disease and diabetes. There are several symptoms:

  o Low levels of HDL
  o High triglyceride levels

o   Raised fasting blood sugar levels
o   Elevated blood pressure
o   Abdominal obesity

The best news? Incorporating a low-carb diet into your life can drastically
reduce all these symptoms. The ketogenic diet has the key to unlock a
much healthier physical life.

- **Therapy for some brain disorders** – There are certain areas of our brains that strictly run on glucose as a fuel. This is the reason behind why our livers produce it from protein if we do not consume carbs. There are bigger portions of our brains, however, that burn through ketones. Think back to Charlie Abraham, who was mentioned earlier in this chapter. In studies, more than half of children who utilized the ketogenic diet had a 50% reduction in seizures. This diet, among other low-carb diets, are being studied as to what its effect is on brain disorders like Parkinson's and Alzheimer's disease.

Risks

Just like with every good thing in the world, there are some risk factors to consider before diving head first on your journey with the ketogenic diet.

- **Fatigue and irritability** – Even though raised ketone levels can drastically improve a few areas regarding your physical quality of life, they are also directly related to feeling tired and having to work harder during physical activities.

- **"Brain fog"** – If you stay on the ketogenic diet long term, there is going to be some major shifting when it comes to the metabolic areas of the body. This can make you moody and somewhat sluggish, which can make you not able to think clearly or adequately focus. Ensure that you are reducing your levels of carb intake at steady levels, not all at once.

- **Lipids may change** – Even though fats on the ketogenic diet are welcomed, if you consume large amounts of saturated fats, your cholesterol levels will begin to increase. Make sure you are consuming healthy fats.

- **Micronutrient deficiencies** – Diets that consists of low-carb foods are more than likely lacking in essential nutrients, such as magnesium, potassium, and iron. You might want to strongly consider finding a high-quality multivitamin to take daily.

- **A possibility of developing ketoacidosis** – If your ketone levels become too out of wack, it may lead to this condition. pH levels within your blood decrease, creating an environment that is high in acidity, which can be threatening for those with diabetes.

- **Muscle loss** – As you consume less energy, your body leans on the help of other tissues as a source of fuel. If you workout heavily while on a diet like the ketogenic, there is the potential for major muscle loss.

Tips to be Successful on the Ketogenic Diet

The main goal when you begin your trek on the ketogenic diet is to keep your body in a constantly stable ketosis state. This is much easier said than done. For those that have personally utilized the diet, many have stated in excitement about how good they feel and look. This chapter is full of fool-proof ways to keep yourself on track as you venture down the ketogenic road!

- **Stay hydrated** – This should be something you do on a daily basis already, but it can sure be a challenge to really stick to it. Drink 32 ounces of water within the first hour your hop out of bed in the morning and strive to consume another 32-48 ounces before the noon hour. Try to drink at least half of your weight in ounces of water or close to your full body weight in ounces of water daily to keep up a good hydration status.

- **Practice the ways of intermittent fasting** – It is a good idea to start reducing your carb intake a couple to a few days before getting down and dirty on the ketogenic diet. Break your day down into two phases:

- o **Building phase** – Amount of time between first and last meal
- o **Cleaning phase** – Amount of time between last and first meal

It is recommended to begin with a 12-16 hour cleaning phase and an 8-12 hour building phase. Your body will adapt to this over time, which then you will be able to move to a 4-6 hour building time paired with an 18-20 hour cleaning phase per day. It will be much simpler to maintain levels of ketosis this way.

- **Consume good salts** – We are constantly reminded to reduce our consumption of sodium. When you undergo a low-carb diet, insulin levels decrease and our kidneys naturally excrete higher levels of sodium which lowers our sodium/potassium ratio in our bodies, which will then need greater need for sodium in our diet.
  - o Consume pumpkin seeds or macadamia nuts as a snack
  - o Eat cucumber or celery, both have natural sodium
  - o Add kelp, nori or dulse to dishes
  - o Add ¼ teaspoon of pink salt to glasses of water

- o   Be generous with amount of pink salt you add to food
- o   Drink organic broth off and on throughout the day

- **Regular exercise** – Daily amounts of high-intensity exercise assists in the activation of glucose molecules known as GLUT-4 that recites information from different areas of the body back to the liver and muscle tissues. This receptor yanks sugar from the bloodstream and uses it as muscle and liver glycogen. Exercising on a regular basis doubles the levels of crucial proteins in both the muscles and liver.

- **Work on improving the mobility of bowels** – No one likes talking about their bowel movements, but if you are constantly constipated, ketosis has a harder time working its magic. Many people struggle with constipation issues while on the ketogenic diet. To help with this, consume some fermented edibles, such as sauerkraut, coconut water, kimchi, etc. It is also recommended to take extra supplements like magnesium. Drinking one fresh green drink per day will also help increase the levels of calcium, magnesium, and potassium in your system, all of which help aid constipation.

- **Don't consume *too* much protein** – Even though it has been strongly stated that the consumption of proteins is recommended as it is required by the ketogenic diet, some people do not know a proper balance and eat too much protein. If you consume too much, your body will change all those amino acids into glucose through the process known as gluconeogenesis. You will probably have to play with the amounts of protein you eat because some people need more or less than others.

  - You should aim for 1 gram of protein per kilogram of body weight. For example, if you weigh 160 pounds that comes out to 2.2 pound per kilogram, which equals about 73 grams of protein. It is best to consume 2-3 servings of 15-50 grams of protein per meal.

- **Choose the carbs you consume wisely** – Even though the ketogenic diet recommends to stay far away from carbs, it is in your best interest to at least consume some good types of carbohydrates, such as starchy veggies and fruits such as limes, lemon, apples, and berries These are especially good if combined within a green protein shake.

- **Utilize MCT oil when you can** – While on the ketogenic diet, the use of high-quality medium chain triglyceride (MCT) is crucial in maintaining the state of ketosis. This is because this oil allows those that consume it to eat more carbs/ proteins and still maintain a good level for ketosis. You can not only cook with this oil but add it into coffee, tea, green drinks, protein shakes and more!

- **Keep stress to a minimum** – Easier said than done, I know. But daily stress will inhibit the process of ketosis to the point of being non-existent. If you are under constant chronic stress, then now may not be the time to undergo the ketogenic diet, but rather an anti-inflammatory, lower carb diet instead.

- **Learn ways to improve the quality of sleep** – If you are not receiving adequate amounts of rest, this is another aspect that can lead to a rise in stress hormones. Ensure that you catch your zzz's in a dark room that you feel comfortable in. It is recommended to receive around 7-9 hours of sleep per night. The more stressed you are, the more sleep you need. Ensure that you are sleeping in a room that is no warmer than 65-70 degrees.

- **Consume some ghee** – Ghee is a grand substitute for butter and is highly recommended on the ketogenic diet. You can use it as normally as you utilize butter.

- **Take Omega-3's** – It is vital that you consume or take Omega-3 vitamins. You should have higher levels of Omega 3's than Omega 6's in your diet. Eating all that oil will cause you harm if your omegas are not properly balanced.

- **Avoid alcohol** – I know, this doesn't sound that fun. But the consumption of alcohol quite literally puts an abrupt stop to your weight loss. Which is worth it: that glass of wine or being able to fit into those skinnier pants?

- **Lemon water is your friend** – Not only is it tasty and pretty darn refreshing, but lemon water actually balances out your pH levels in your body, creating a better environment for ketosis to properly thrive.

- **Avoid "sugar-free" products** –Even though it sounds better for you, try to avoid products that say "sugar-free" or "light" because these more than likely have more carbs than their original counterparts.

- **Avoid low-fat** – While on the ketogenic diet, you should steer clear and not waste your precious time with anything that is low in fat. You need to have high percentages of fat in your diet in order to maintain an adequate and healthy balance. Otherwise, the protein you consume may be converted into sugars too.

Ketogenic Breakfast Recipes

Taking the time to prepare and consume a nice, low-carb breakfast to begin the course of your day can truly set the tone for how you will feel and consume other meals throughout the remainder of the day. It is important to ensure that your body and tummy are satisfied, fueled and ready to conquer what lies ahead of you! These ketogenic breakfast recipes will be sure to hit the spot!

Fat-Burning Vanilla Smoothie

Calories – 650
Fat – 64 grams
Protein – 12 grams
Net Carbs – 4 grams

Makes 1 serving

What's in it:

- 3 drops of liquid stevia
- ½ tsp. vanilla extract
- 1 tbsp. MCT or coconut oil
- 4 ice cubes
- ¼ c. water
- ½ c. full-fat mascarpone cheese

- 2 large egg yolks
- Optional: Whipped cream

How it's made:

- Combine stevia, vanilla, coconut oil, ice, water, creamed coconut milk, mascarpone cheese and eggs yolks in a blender, pulsing until smooth in texture
- Top with whipped cream if desired and enjoy!

<u>Blackberry Egg Bake</u>

Calories – 144
Fat – 10 grams
Protein – 8.5 grams
Net Carbs – 2 grams

Makes 4 servings

What's in it:
- ½ c. fresh blackberries
- 1 tsp. finely chopped fresh rosemary
- Zest of ½ an orange
- 1/3 tsp. fine sea salt
- ¼ tsp. vanilla
- 1 tsp. freshly grated ginger
- 3 tbsp. coconut flour
- 1 tbsp. melted butter
- 5 large eggs

How it's made:

- Ensure the oven is preheated to 350 degrees and proceed to adequately grease 4 ramekins
- In a blender, pour in all ingredients minus rosemary and blackberries. Then blend until mixture is smooth in texture
- Add in rosemary and pulse until combined
- Divide the blended mixture in-between all 4 ramekins
- Add blackberries on top of each ramekin
- Place ramekins on baking sheet and back for 15-20 minutes until the egg mixture puffs up and is cooked
- Cool for 15-30 minutes before serving. Can be consumed either in or out of ramekins

Coconut Pancakes

575 Calories
51 grams of Fat
19 grams of Protein
3.5 grams of Net Carbs

Makes 2 pancakes

What's in it:

- 2-5 tbsp. maple syrup
- ¼ c. unsweetened shredded coconut

- 1 pinch of salt
- ½ tbsp. erythritol
- 1 tsp. cinnamon
- 1 tbsp. almond flour
- 2 ounces of cream cheese
- 2 large eggs

How it's made:

- In a mixing bowl, crack and whisk together eggs. Proceed in adding cream cheese, whisking until well combined and creamy in texture
- Then whisk in salt, erythritol, cinnamon and almond flour
- Add half the pancake batter into a pan over medium heat. Cook until edges start to brown and appear dry, which takes around 3-5 minutes. (These are meant to be big pancakes so be patient with cooking time.)
- Flip pancake and cook opposing side for 1 minute
- Put on plate and sprinkle with shredded coconut
- Feel free to top pancakes with syrup or other toppings

Peanut Butter Chocolate Chip Muffins

530 Calories
41 grams of Fat
15 grams of Protein

4.5 grams of Net Carbs

Makes 6 servings

What's in it:

- 2 large eggs
- 1/3 c. almond milk
- 1/3 c. peanut butter
- 1 tsp. baking powder
- 1 pinch of salt
- ½ c. erythritol
- 1 c. almond flour
- ½. c. cacao nibs or sugar-free chocolate chips

How it's made:

- Ensure over is preheated to 350 degrees. Grease a muffin tin or add cupcake liners to a muffin tin
- Combine all dry ingredients together in a large bowl, except cacao nibs. Stir until thoroughly mixed
- Add almond milk and peanut butter to dry mixture and combine well
- Adding in 1 egg at a time, ensure to stir until each is thoroughly mixed in
- Fold in cacao nibs
- Evenly distribute batter into 6 muffins
- Bake for 15 minutes
- Let them cool and enjoy with maple syrup or butter

Low-Carb Green Breakfast Smoothie

375 Calories
Fat – 25 grams
Protein – 30 grams
Net Carbs – 4 grams

Makes 1 serving

What's in it:

- 10 drops of liquid stevia
- 1 tbsp. of coconut oil
- 50 grams of avocado
- 50 grams of celery
- 50 grams of cucumber
- 1 ounce of spinach
- 1 ½ c. almond milk
- 1 scoop protein powder (30 grams)
- ½ tsp. chia seeds for garnish
- Optional: 1 tsp. matcha powder

How it's made:

- Blend spinach and almond milk in a blender, enough to break spinach down so that there is enough room for remaining ingredients
- Pour in rest of ingredients into blender and blend for 1 minute or until creamy in texture
- Add a teaspoon of matcha powder for a nice kick if desired

- Pour into a glass and top with chia seeds

Butter Coffee

230 Calories
25 grams of Fat
0 grams of Protein
0 grams of Net Carbs

Makes 1 serving

What's in it:

- 1 tbsp. coconut oil
- 1 tbsp. grass fed butter
- 2 tbsp. coffee
- 1 c. water

How it's made:

- Make a cup of coffee in whatever style you desire and suits you
- In a blender, mix together brewed coffee, butter, and coconut oil. Blend for about 10 seconds. It should be creamy and light in color
- Pour into your favorite coffee mug and enjoy! Feel free to add other ingredients like whipped cream or cinnamon

Shakshuka

490 Calories
Fat – 34 grams

Protein – 35 grams
Net Carbs – 4 grams

Makes 1 serving

What's in it:

- Fresh basil
- Pepper
- Salt
- 1/8 tsp. cumin
- 1 ounce of feta cheese
- 4 eggs
- 1 chili pepper
- 1 c. marinara sauce

How it's made:

- Ensure over is preheated to 400 degrees
- In a small skillet over medium heat, heat up marinara sauce and chopped chili pepper. Let cook for about 5 minutes within the sauce
- Crack and put eggs directly into marinara sauce
- Sprinkle feta cheese over eggs, then proceed to season with cumin, salt, and pepper
- Using an over mitt, transfer skillet from stovetop to oven
- Bake for about 10 minutes
- Once eggs appear cooked but still have a runny consistency, take the skillet out of

the oven. Chop up basil and sprinkle over shakshuka

- Eat right from skillet or put on plate

Eggs Benedict a la Oopsie

497 Calories
38.1 grams of Fat
30.3 grams of Protein
2.4 grams of Net Carbs

Makes 2 servings

What's in it:

Eggs Benedict

- 1 tsp. chives
- 1 tbsp. white vinegar
- 4 slices of Canadian bacon
- 4 eggs
- 4 Oopsie rolls

Hollandaise Sauce

- 1 pinch of paprika
- 1 pinch of salt
- 1 tsp. lemon juice
- 2 tbsp. butter
- 2 eggs yolks

How it's made:

- Separate 2 eggs and whisk together yolks until they double in volume. Add a bit of lemon juice
- Boil about 1 inch of water
- Melt some butter to add to sauce later
- Utilizing a double boiler, whisk in lemony egg yolks at fast speed. They should become thicker the more you whisk
- Pour in melted butter slowly while whisking.
- Take sauce away from heat, season it with paprika and salt. If it cool and thickens a bit too much, just add a touch of water and whisk it to make it spoonable once again.
- For eggs, boil about 3 inches of water, reduce to simmer, add salt and tbsp. of white vinegar
- With a wooden spoon, make a whirlpool in water by stirring a few times in one direction
- Crack an egg into a cup and lower into whirlpool gently. Don't drop egg in, lower cup and let it out
- Cook egg for about 2-4 minutes, you want a runny consistency
- Lift egg out with a spatula and let rest on a plate lined in paper towels.
- Repeat with remaining eggs
- Fry Canadian bacon however you like

- Top Oopsie rolls with bacon and place poached eggs on each slice of bacon
- Dollop about a tbsp. of hollandaise sauce onto eggs, season as desired with salt and pepper and sprinkle chives before serving

Egg Clouds with Bacon Weave

172 Calories
Fat – 12 grams
Protein – 14 grams
Net Carbs – 0 grams

Makes 2 servings

What's in it:

- ¼ tsp. cayenne
- ¼ tsp. pepper
- ½ tsp. garlic powder
- ½ tsp. salt
- 2 eggs
- 6 strips of bacon

How it's made:

- Ensure oven is preheated to 350 degrees
- Take 3 strips of bacon and fold in half lengthwise. Cut along fold to ensure halves are the same length

- Lay 3 half length strips of bacon parallel to each other on a baking sheet and fold middle strip over
- Place a strip perpendicular to the 3 and fold back over. Fold two outer strips over
- Place another strip of bacon in the center perpendicularly, flipping middle strip over to weave
- Place the final strip of bacon on and flip back over.
- Separate 2 eggs and save yolks in a separate bowl. Try your best to keep yolks intact. In a mixing bowl, place egg whites.
- Whisk egg whites together with electric hand mixer for roughly 5 minutes. Whites should transform into a white, thick foam and should form stiff peaks
- Then add garlic powder and salt and whisk in.
- Spoon seasoned eggs whites onto bacon weaves to create a cloud. Make a dip in each "cloud" to put egg yolks in
- Bake for about 10 minutes until bacon is sizzling and clouds are golden
- Enjoy!

Low-Carb Smoothie Bowl

570 Calories
Fat – 35 grams
Protein – 35 grams
Net Carbs – 4 grams

Makes 1 serving

What's in it:

Smoothie Base

- 2 ice cubes
- 1 scoop of low-carb protein powder
- 1 tbsp. coconut oil
- 2 tbsp. heavy cream
- ½ c. almond milk
- 1 c. spinach

Toppings

- 1 tsp. chia seeds
- 1 tbsp. shredded coconut
- 4 walnuts
- 4 raspberries

How it's made:

- In a blender, mix together spinach, almond milk, cream, coconut oil, and ice. Blend until all ingredients are combined and have an even consistency
- Pour blended mixture into a bowl of choice
- Arrange toppings or throw them in and mix all together
- Enjoy!

Ketogenic Lunch Recipes

Lunch time is not only a break during the course of your work day but also time to take in some sunshine and enjoy your break with an afternoon, low-carb lunch! These recipes will be sure to get you through those lunchie-munchies and satisfy you until snack or dinner time!

Low-Carb Chipotle Fish Tacos

300 Calories
Fat – 20 grams
Protein – 24 grams
Net Carbs – 7 grams

Makes 4 servings

What's in it:

- 4 low-carb tortillas
- 1 pound of haddock fillets
- 2 tbsp. mayo
- 2 tbsp. Butter
- 4 ounces of chipotle pepper in adobo sauce
- 2 pressed cloves of garlic
- 1 chopped jalapeño pepper
- ½ diced yellow onion
- 2 tbsp. olive oil

How it's made:

- Fry diced onion in a tall pan with oil on medium-high heat until translucent in color, which takes roughly 5 minutes
- Reduce heat and add in garlic and jalapeño and continue to cook, ensuring that you stir. Cook for another 2 minutes.
- Chop chipotles and pour them in with adobo sauce
- Add fish fillets, mayo and butter to pan
- Mix everything together for around 8 minutes until fish is cooked
- To make shells: fry tortilla in a pan, frying 2 minutes per side on high heat.
- Let shells cool and fill them with fish mixture

<u>Chicken Salad Stuffed Avocado</u>

570 Calories
Fat – 45 grams
Protein – 29 grams
Net Carbs – 5 grams

Makes 1 serving

What's in it:

- 1/3 c. sour cream
- 1 medium avocado
- 1 stalk of celery

- 1 tbsp. diced red onion
- 3 ounces of cooked and shredded chicken breast

How it's made:

- Cook chicken breast on low heat until cooked thoroughly, then shred using two forks
- In a bowl, mix together celery, red onion, and chicken
- Cut and pit an avocado. Place some of scooped out avocado into bowl
- Add sour cream, salt, and pepper
- Tossed all ingredients together and spoon back into avocado halves
- Enjoy!

Low-Carb Chicken Quesadilla

654 Calories
Fat – 43 grams
Protein – 52 grams
Net Carbs – 7 grams

Makes 1 serving

What's in it:

- ¼ tsp. salt
- ¼ tsp. garlic powder
- ¼ tsp. crushed red pepper
- ¼ tsp. dried basil

- 1 low-carb wrap
- 1 tsp. chopped jalapeño
- ½ thinly sliced avocado
- 2.5 ounces of grilled chicken breast
- 3 ounces of pepper jack cheese

How it's Made:

- Grill chicken breast with spices
- Place wrap onto a frying pan that is placed over medium-high heat
- Cook each side of wrap for 2 minutes and then begin laying out pepper jack. Ensure that you are not placing cheese too close to edges of wrap
- Add chicken breast, jalapeño, and sliced avocado to half of wrap
- Fold over wrap with a spatula and then press to flatten. The melted cheese will act as glue to hold wrap together
- Take out of the pan and cut into a third. Eat with sour cream and salsa

<u>Cheesy Spinach Rolls with Apple Slaw</u>

670 Calories
Fat – 67 grams
Protein – 32 grams
Net Carbs – 16 grams

Makes 16-20 rolls

What's in it:

Crust

- ½ tsp. sea salt
- 2 eggs
- 6 tbsp. coconut flour
- ½ c. almond flour
- 2 ½ c. shredded mozzarella

Filling

- 1 pinch sea salt
- ¼ c. grated parmesan
- 4 ounces of cream cheese
- 6 ounces of spinach

Topping

- ¼ tsp. sea salt
- ¼ c. mayo
- 1 apple
- ¾ c. coleslaw salad mix

How it's made:

- Ensure oven is preheated to 350 degrees
- Wilt spinach leaves in a large pan over high heat with a bit of oil
- Once leaves are wilted, add cream cheese and parmesan, stirring

everything together until combined and melty

- Remove from source of heat and then set to the side
- To make crust: Pop mozzarella in microwave for 30 seconds or until it is pliable
- Add almond and coconut flours and mix. Add eggs and salt and combine. Mixing will take a few minutes
- Lay ball of cheese dough on a piece of parchment paper. Then lay a secondary sheet of parchment over top and flatten out dough with a rolling pin until it is around 1/8" in thickness
- Cut dough into 3"x4" rectangles
- Add about ½ tsp. of spinach mixture to one side of dough rectangle. Roll dough over carefully, rolling it into a cigar-like shape.
- Repeat this until you have used all dough and spinach mixture
- Transfer rolls to a baking sheet that is lined and greased. Bake rolls for 16-18 minutes until lightly golden. Let cool for about 10 minutes

- To make apple slaw: Grate 1 apple into a bowl and add in cole slaw mix, along with mayo and salt. Combine and chill until ready.
- Once rolls are cooled, top them with slaw and enjoy!

Chipotle Steak Bowl

620 Calories
50 grams of Fat
3 grams of Protein
5.5 grams of Net Carbs

Makes 4 servings

What's in it:

- A splash of Tabasco sauce
- 1 handful of fresh cilantro
- 1 c. sour cream
- 4 ounces of pepper jack cheese
- 1 guacamole recipe
- Salt and pepper, to taste
- 16 ounces of skirt steak

How it's made:

- In a heated-up cast iron skillet, season skirt steak with salt and pepper and cook each side up to 3-4 minutes on high heat. Let rest while you prepare guacamole
- Slice steak against the grain then cut into bite-sized strips and divide into 4 even portions
- Shred pepper jack cheese and top each portion of meat
- Add ¼ c. of guac to each portion, followed by a ¼ c. of sour cream

- Splash with Tabasco sauce and top with fresh cilantro

Lamb Meatballs with Cauliflower Pilaf

495 Calories
41 grams of Fat
27 grams of Protein
3.5 grams of Net Carbs

Makes 4 servings

What's in it:

Cauliflower Rice

- Salt and pepper
- 200 grams of cauliflower florets

Meatballs

- 1 tsp. paprika
- 1 tsp. pepper
- 1 tsp. garlic powder
- 1 tsp. fennel seed
- 1 tsp. salt
- 1 large egg
- 1 pound of ground lamb

Other ingredients

- 4 ounces of goat cheese
- 1 tbsp. lemon zest
- 1 bunch of roughly chopped mint leaves
- 4 grams of minced garlic
- ½ of a chopped yellow onion
- 2 tbsp. coconut oil

How it's made:
- In a food processor, pulse cauliflower until it resembles the appearance of rice
- In a lightly oiled pan, cook cauliflower rice for 8 minutes, season with salt and pepper to get desired taste
- Combine lamb, eggs, and spices in a large bowl. Using hands, mix well and then form 12-15 meatballs. Set aside
- In a skillet, cook onion in coconut oil over medium heat until onion is translucent in color
- Add garlic and sauté until you smell its fragrance
- Add meatballs to pan, ensuring they get cooked on all sides. Cook until there is no longer any pink color visible and they are firm to the touch
- Divide up cauliflower rice into 4 portions
- Add meatballs to each portion of rice and top with mint leaves, lemon zest, and crumbled goat cheese

Low-Carb Lemon Garlic Shrimp Pasta

360 Calories
Fat – 21 grams
Protein – 36 grams
Net Carbs – 3.5 grams

Makes 4 servings

What's in it:

- Fresh basil
- Salt and pepper
- ½ tsp. paprika
- 1 pound of large raw shrimp
- ½ lemon
- 4 garlic cloves
- 2 tbsp. olive oil
- 2 tbsp. butter
- 2 bags of angel hair pasta

How it's made:

- Get a pot of water to start boiling and in the meantime, rinse angel hair noodles with cool water. Then boil for 2 minutes
- In a dry, hot pan over medium heat, dry roast noodles to evaporate excess water. Once dry, set aside as you prepare remainder of recipe
- In the same pan, heat up butter and olive oil. Crush garlic cloves and add to butter and oil. Cook all until fragrant but not brown in color

- Slice up lemons into rounds and add them and shrimp to garlic. Cook for 3 minutes per side
- When shrimp is opaque in color, add noodles to pan and season to desired taste with paprika, salt, and pepper
- Mix up all ingredients to ensure that noodles are coated evenly
- Serve with fresh basil sprinkled on top. Enjoy!

Ultimate Mexican Casserole

250 Calories
Fat – 14 grams
Protein – 19 grams
Net Carbs – 6 grams

Makes 6 servings

What's in it:

- Fresh cilantro
- 1 freshly sliced jalapeño
- 2 low-carb tortillas
- 1 c. shredded pepper jack cheese
- 1 pound of boneless skinless chicken thighs
- 1 c. red enchilada sauce
- 4 ounces of cream cheese
- ¼ c. heavy cream
- ½ medium chopped white onion
- 2 chopped chipotle peppers

- 2 freshly chopped jalapeños
- 1 tbsp. olive oil

How it's made:

- Ensure oven is preheated to 350 degrees
- In a large skillet that is properly oiled over medium-high heat, cook diced onion, chipotle peppers, and jalapeños. Sauté for 5 minutes until your onion is fragrant and translucent in terms of color
- Add in cream cheese and heavy cream. Stir everything together until cream cheese is completely melted
- Add shredded chicken and enchilada sauce, stir well to combine
- In a 13x9 lightly greased baking pan, place 2 tortillas side by side
- Pour chicken mixture over tortillas and top it all with shredded cheese. Add sliced jalapeños on top
- With foil, cover baking dish and bake for 15 minutes
- Take out of oven, remove aluminum foil and bake for another 15 minutes, until cheese is lightly browned
- Serve along with cilantro

Easy Buffalo Wings

620 Calories
Fat – 46 grams
Protein – 48 grams
Net Carbs – 1 gram

Makes 2 servings

What's in it:

- Paprika
- Garlic powder
- Salt and pepper
- 2 tbsp. butter
- ½ c. Frank's Red Hot Sauce
- 6 chicken wings
- *Optional: Cayenne*

How it's made:

- Break chicken wings up into wingettes and drumettes and discard the tips. Pour Frank's Red Hot Sauce over wings, just enough to coat them
- Season wings and toss to ensure good coverage. Chill wings for about an hour or so
- Turn broiler on high and place oven rack 6 inches from broiler. Line a sheet with foil. Lay our chicken wings so each has enough space for the flame to reach the sides as well
- Let cook in the broiler for 8 minutes. Color on top should be a nice darkened brown

- While chicken wings are broiling, melt 2 tbsp. of butter and stir in rest of hot sauce. Season with cayenne pepper if you so choose. Take sauce off heat once butter is completely melted
- Take wings out of broiler and flip them and proceed to cook for another 6-8 minutes
- Once browned on all side, place wings in a mixing bowl and pour in hot sauce and butter mixture to coat them. Toss evenly and serve!

Ketogenic Snack Recipes

We all get the dreaded hunger pain towards the middle of the afternoon and many of us do not fulfill it in a very healthy manner. We scrounge around desperately trying to find something to satisfy our snack-driven taste-buds but to no avail! But with these great snacks, you will not have to fear the dreaded afternoon hunger strike again!

<u>Snacks that Require no Prep Time</u>

- Pickles
- Sugar-free jello
- Sardines
- Avocados
- Cherry Tomatoes
- Nuts
- Cocoa nibs
- Jerky
- String cheese
- Seaweed
- Dark chocolate
- Hummus
- Seeds
- Pork rinds

Green Bean Fries

113 Calories
6 grams of Fat
9 grams of Protein
2.5 grams of Net Carbs

Makes 4 servings

What's in it:

- ¼ tsp. black pepper
- ½ tsp. pink Himalayan salt
- 2/3 c. grated parmesan
- 1 large egg
- 12 ounces of green beans
- *½ tsp. garlic powder (optional)*
- *½ tsp. paprika (optional)*

How it's made:

- Ensure oven is preheated to 400 degrees
- Ensure that your green beans are dry and ends are snipped
- On a plate, combine seasonings with grated Parmesan cheese and mix together
- In a bowl, whisk an egg. Drench green beans in beaten egg and allow excess egg to drop off beans for a dew seconds per handful

- Press green beans in parmesan cheese mixture and sprinkle cheese over them. Toss gently
- On a greased, large baking sheet, place green beans evenly. Bake for around 10 minutes or until beans are golden in terms of color.
- Let green beans cool so that you can consume with fingers. Serve alongside spicy mayo or ranch

Bacon-Wrapped Jalapeño Poppers

225 Calories
Fat – 18 grams
Protein – 10 grams
Net Carbs – 3 grams

Makes 4 servings

What's in it:

- 1 tsp. paprika
- 1 tsp. salt
- ¼ c. shredded cheddar cheese
- 4 ounces of cream cheese
- 16 strips bacon
- 16 fresh jalapenos

How it's made:

- Ensure that your oven is preheated 350 degrees

- Slice bacon in half so that you have 16 pieces cut into half length
- Slice off ends of the jalapeños. Slice each pepper in half length-wise and ensure that you remove all seeds and innards
- Mix cheddar and cream cheese together
- Take the cheese mixture and proceed to fill each jalapeño half
- Engulf each jalapeño half with bacon
- Place jalapeño peppers on a foil-lined baking sheet. Ensure there is room between each popper. Back 20-25 minutes
- Add paprika, salt, and other spices to taste and enjoy

Coconut Butter Cup Fat Bombs

260 Calories
26 grams of Fat
3 grams of Protein
0.5 grams of Carbs

Makes 4 servings

What's in it:

- 1 pinch of salt
- 4 tsp. coconut butter
- 2 tbsp. erythritol
- 4 tbsp. coconut oil
- 4 tbsp. cocoa powder

How it's made:

- Mix together erythritol, cocoa powder, and coconut oil, stirring until there are no clumps left. Add a pinch of salt
- Pour about half the chocolate mixture evenly into 4 silicone cupcake molds. Tilt molds so that chocolate mixture coats edges. Freeze for around 5 minutes
- Spoon a tsp. of coconut butter into each mold. Tap plate of molds on a counter to ensure that the coconut butter spreads out evenly over chocolate later. Place in freezer again for a few more minutes
- Take remaining chocolate and cover the now hardened coconut butter. Freeze for 5 more minutes and you are ready to enjoy

Crunchy Kale Chips

180 Calories
Fat – 16 grams
Protein – 4 grams
Net Carbs – 3 grams

Makes 2 servings

What's in it:

- 1 tsp. crushed red pepper
- 1 tsp. salt

- 1 tsp. garlic powder
- 2 tbsp. Parmesan cheese
- 2 tbsp. olive oil
- 1 bunch of kale

How it's made:

- Ensure oven is preheated to 350 degrees
- Wash and thoroughly dry your bunch of kale
- Rip kale into pieces, either leaving stem on our cutting it off
- Pour oil of choice over kale and add seasoning
- Toss kale and seasonings with hands to combine thoroughly. Almost every leaf should be shiny with oil
- On a cookie sheet, disperse kale leaves evenly
- Bake kale for 8 minutes. Check on them periodically. If chips are still soft, continue to bake in 2-minute intervals. Average baking time is 12 minutes
- When crunchy to your liking, take them out and put in a bowl
- Get to snacking!

Cheddar-Wrapped Taco Rolls

491 Calories
Fat – 35 grams
Protein – 37 grams

Net Carbs -2 grams

Makes 3 servings

What's in it:

Crust

- 2 c. shredded cheddar cheese

Topping

- 2 tsp. Sriracha mayo or taco sauce
- ½ of an avocado, chopped
- ¼ c. chopped tomatoes
- 1 c. taco meat (already cooked and seasoned

How it's made:

- Ensure oven is preheated to 400 degrees
- With parchment paper, line a baking sheet, ensuring that you leave room on sides to life cheese up when done
- Grease parchment paper lightly, focusing especially on the edges
- Sprinkle shredded cheddar cheese to where the bottom of the pan is covered in a thin layer. You may have to use more than 2 cups if necessary
- Stick in oven and bake for around 15 minutes until cheese is bubbly and starts to turn brown in terms of color

- Take tray out of oven
- Add taco meat, then bake for another 5-10 minutes until hot
- While baking, in a small bowl mix together rest of toppings until combined
- Remove sheet from oven and utilizing the sides of parchment, pull off cheese from pan
- Add on cold toppings in a single layer
- Using a pizza cutter, cut top to bottom to make 3-4 slices
- Roll each slice from bottom to top

Supreme Pizza Rolls

117 Calories
Fat – 8 grams
Protein – 11 grams
Net Carbs – 2 grams

Makes 6 servings

What's in it:

- ¼ c. pizza sauce
- 2 sliced grape tomatoes
- ½ c. cooked and crumbled sausage
- 2 tbsp. chopped white onions
- ¼ c. chopped green and red peppers
- 1 tsp. pizza seasoning
- 2 c. mozzarella cheese

How it's made:

- Ensure that your oven is preheated to 400 degrees
- With parchment paper, line a baking sheet, ensuring that you leave extra room, especially along the sides so you can lift it out while hot
- Use a bit of olive oil to rub down parchment
- Sprinkle cheese on a baking sheet. Should be a single layer that covers the bottom
- Sprinkle pizza seasoning over cheese
- Stick in oven and bake for 20 minutes up to the point that cheese starts to turn brown in terms of color.
- Remove from oven and add sliced tomatoes, red and green peppers, onions and sausage. Then drizzle tomato sauce over all ingredients
- Pop back in oven and bake for an additional 10 minutes
- Take out of oven and remove pizza by lifting sides of parchment paper
- Looking at your pizza horizontally, cut in 6 strips top to bottom. Then roll strips from top to bottom
- Allow to cool for a couple minutes then enjoy

Crispy Cheddar Cheese Chips

Makes 4 servings

What's in it:

- ¼ tsp. chili powder
- ¼ tsp. paprika
- ¼ tsp. cumin
- ¼ tsp. garlic powder
- ½ tsp. onion powder
- ½ tsp. sea salt
- 4 c. shredded cheddar cheese (or any blend you prefer)

How it's made:

- Ensure oven is preheated to 400 degrees
- With parchment paper, line a baking sheet, ensuring that there is adequate room along the edges that will allow you to pick it up when hot
- Combine cheese and spices in a bowl
- Spread out cheese mixture evenly onto baking sheet
- Bake for 20 minutes or until cheese is visibly crunchy
- Take out of the oven
- Using parchment paper, lift out of baking sheet

- Allow to cool for at least one minute and proceed to use a pizza cutter to cut cheese into triangles

Ketogenic Dinner Recipes

These keto-inspired dinner recipes will have your family and friends totally delighted and they will have no idea that what they are eating is pretty darn healthy as well! The recipes in this chapter will be sure to satisfy your end of the day cravings as well as hone your skills in the kitchen. Enjoy!

One-Pan Italian Sausage Dinner Skillet

500 Calories
38 grams of Fat
30 grams of Protein
4.5 grams of Net Carbs

Makes 2 servings

What's in it:

- ½ tsp. red pepper
- ¼ tsp. salt
- ½ tsp. basil
- ½ tsp. oregano
- ¼ c. shredded mozzarella
- ¼ c. Parmesan cheese
- ½ c. vodka sauce
- 4 ounces of mushrooms
- 1 tbsp. white onion
- 3 sausage links

How it's made:

- Ensure oven is preheated to 350 degrees
- Heat up a cast iron skillet over medium heat. When it begins to start smoking, add sausage links and cook thoroughly
- Slice onion and mushrooms while sausage cooks
- When sausage is almost done, remove from skillet. Pour in onions and mushrooms and allow them to brown
- Cut sausage links into rounds that are around ½" in thickness and add them back to skillet. Season sausage and veggie mixture
- Pour vodka sauce and add in parmesan cheese. Combine thoroughly
- Place skillet in oven for 15 minutes. Sprinkle mozzarella cheese in right before it is done so it has time to melt
- Eat right from skillet!

<u>Turkey Ramen with Zoodles</u>

123 Calories
3 grams of Fat
15 grams of Protein
7 grams of Net Carbs

Makes 2 servings

What's in it:

- Salt, to taste
- 2 eggs
- 1 c. sliced shitake mushrooms
- 1 large zucchini
- 4 thick cuts of turkey
- Hot sauce
- 1 tbsp. soy sauce
- 1 tsp. ginger paste
- 1 tbsp. minced garlic
- ½ c. sliced carrots
- ½ c. chopped scallions
- 4 c. turkey stock or bone broth

How it's made:

- Mix together hot sauce, soy sauce, ginger, garlic, carrots, scallions and turkey stock in a crock pot
- Cook on low for about 4 hours
- Add salt to broth if desired
- In a medium sized pot, add eggs and cover with water
- Once water begins to boil, turn off heat and let eggs sit for 5-6 minutes
- Add turkey and mushrooms to your crock pot and cook 5-10 minutes until heated through
- Utilizing a spiralizer, cut off the ends of your zucchini and push through the machine to create zucchini noodles. Add to bowls and set aside

- Using a pair of tongs, remove turkey and mushrooms from crock pot and divide them evenly among portions. Then pour broth over zoodles. Let sit for one minute.
- Crack your eggs and slice your boiled eggs in half and place over top of zoodle mixture. Sprinkle the rest of your scallion over top for a nice-looking garnish. Salt and pepper to your liking

Easy Spicy Crock Pot Double Beef Stew

222 Calories
7 grams of Fat
27 grams of Protein
9 grams of Net Carbs

Makes 6 servings

What's in it:

- 1 tbsp. Worcestershire sauce
- Salt (to taste)
- 2 tsp. hot sauce
- 1 c. beef broth
- 1 tbsp. chili mix
- 2 14.5 ounce cans of chili ready diced tomatoes
- 1 ½ pounds of beef stew meat

How it's made:

- Ensure that your crock pot is turned to high
- Pour in all ingredients into pot and mix well
- Cook for 6 hours on high
- When 6 hours is up, pull apart and break up meat with a fork inside pot
- Add salt now if you feel like it needs it
- Cook for another 2 hours on low and serve

<u>Butter Coffee Rubbed Tri-Tip Steak</u>

What's in it:

- 2 tbsp. olive oil
- ½ tbsp. garlic powder
- 1 package of coffee blocks
- 1 tsp. course ground black pepper
- 2 Tri-tip steaks

How it's made:

- Let meat sit at room temperature for around 20 minutes. Proceed to tenderize meat with a mallet if desired
- Combine all steak ingredients minus the meat in a bowl. Mix well.
- Rub mixture onto steaks. Ensure that you coat the bottom, top, and sides all well

- Over medium-high heat, heat up a skillet with olive oil
- Put steaks in skillet and cook on one side for 5 minutes. Flip and cook another side for another 5 minutes or until meat is 140 degrees for medium rare
- Remove meat from pan and let it sit in juices for at least 1 minute. The longer you wait, the better
- Cut steak into slices against the grain and enjoy

Roasted Red Pepper and Garlic Stuffed Mozzarella Chicken

Makes 2 servings

What's in it:

- 1 tbsp. freshly chopped oregano
- Freshly ground pepper
- Garlic salt
- 1 tbsp. all-purpose chicken seasoning
- 1 roasted pepper (sliced in half long ways)
- 6 cloves of garlic
- 8 small herb marinated mozzarella balls
- 10 fresh basil leaves
- 2 boneless, skinless chicken breasts
- 2 tbsp. extra virgin olive oil

How it's made:

- Ensure oven is preheated to 400 degrees
- Take chicken breasts and tenderize them a bit and then butterfly cut them
- Put fresh basil in each breast and top with mozzarella balls
- Squeeze garlic cloves between them
- Top with red pepper on top of mozzarella
- Drizzle marinated oil over top along with a good dose of garlic salt and ground pepper
- Sprinkle chopped oregano over entire dish
- Place all in a glass baking dish
- Bake uncovered for 40 minutes or until internal temperature is 180 degrees

<u>Low Carb Shepard's Pie</u>

469 Calories
39 grams of Fat
23 grams of Protein
6 grams of Net Carbs

Makes 6 servings

What's in it:

- 1 tsp. dried thyme
- ¼ c. grated parmesan

- 1 c. shredded cheese
- 1 c. heavy cream
- 2 12 ounce packages of riced cauliflower (cooked and then drained well)
- 1 c. chopped tomatoes
- ½ c. chopped celery
- 3 cloves of minced garlic
- ¼ c. chopped yellow onion
- 1 pound of ground turkey, beef or lamb
- ¼ c. oil

How it's made:

- Ensure oven is preheated to 350 degrees
- In a large skillet, heat up oil. Then proceed in adding celery, garlic, onions and ground meat. Sauté until the meat is totally browned.
- Once meat is cooked, turn off heat and pour in tomatoes. Stir well. Transfer mixture to casserole dish that is around 10x7 inches
- Blend cauliflower, thyme, cream and cheeses in a food processor until the mixture looks like mashed potatoes
- Spread cauliflower mixture over meat within the casserole dish
- Bake for 35-40 minutes
- Let cool a bit before serving

5 Ingredient Avocado Lime Salmon

420 Calories
27 grams of Fat
37 grams of Protein
5 grams of Net Carbs

Makes 2 servings

What's in it:

- 100 grams of cauliflower
- 2 tbsp. diced red onion
- ½ lime
- 1 avocado
- 2 6-ounce salmon fillets

How it's made:

- In a food processor, pulse cauliflower to make it into a rice-like texture. Then cook in a lightly oiled, covered pan for about 8 minutes
- Blend together lime juice, red onion and avocado in a food processor until it is smooth and creamy in texture
- In a heated skillet with oil, cook salmon fillets skin side down for 4-5 minutes. Make sure to season with salt and pepper during course of cooking
- Flip salmon fillets over and cook additional 4-5 minutes on opposing side

- Once cooked, serve salmon over a bed of cauliflower rice with a nice dollop of avocado lime sauce. Enjoy!

Low Carb Sesame Chicken

520 Calories
36 grams of Fat
45 grams of Protein
4 grams of Net Carbs

Makes 2 servings

What's in it:

Coating and Chicken

- Salt and pepper
- 1 tbsp. toasted sesame seed oil
- 1 pound of chicken thighs, cut into bite-sized pieces
- 1 tbsp. corn starch
- 1 egg

Sesame Sauce

- ¼ tsp. xanthan gum
- 2 tbsp. sesame seeds
- 1 clove of garlic
- 1 tbsp. vinegar
- 2 tbsp. Sukrin Gold
- 1 tbsp. toasted sesame seed oil
- 2 tbsp. soy sauce

How it's made:

- To create batter, combine a tbsp. of corn starch with a large egg. Whisk together well and then add in your bite sized pieces of chicken thighs. Ensure they are all evenly coated
- In a large pan, heat up a tbsp. of toasted sesame seed oil and then pour in chicken pieces. Ensure to leave a bit of room between pieces. If you have to do multiple batches, that is fine. The goal is to fry, not steam chicken
- While flipping chicken during frying, be gentle as to not tear off delicious breading. Then your sesame sauce won't stick later on
- While chicken is cooking, make sesame sauce by mixing together all sauce ingredients and whisking well
- Once the chicken is totally cooked through, add sesame sauce to the pan and combine. Let cook for another 5 minutes
- When sauce is thick and heated through, take chicken out of pan and pour it on top of a bed of cooked broccoli
- Serve with a sprinkle of sesame seeds and green onion

Rosemary Apple Pork Chops

485 Calories
41 grams of Fat
25 grams of Protein
4 grams of Net Carbs

Makes 2 servings

What's in it:

Pork Chops

- 4 sprigs of rosemary
- ½ apple
- Paprika
- Salt and pepper
- 2 tbsp. olive oil
- 4 pork chops

Apple Cider Vinaigrette

- 2 tbsp. olive oil
- Salt and pepper
- 1 tbsp. Sugar-free maple syrup
- 1 tbsp. lemon juice
- 2 tbsp. apple cider vinegar

How it's made:

- While you prep your pork chops, heat up a cast iron skillet in a 400-degree oven

- Pat pork chops down with a paper town to dry them and rub olive oil and seasonings on meat
- Take skillet out of oven and set on stovetop over high heat
- Sear each side of your chops for about 2 minutes per side
- Lay apple slices and rosemary on top of chops. Place skillet in the oven for about 10 minutes to complete cooking
- While pork chops are finishing cooking, create apple cider vinaigrette. Mix all vinaigrette ingredients together and combine well. Add oil in as your last ingredient. Slowly pour oil in while rapidly whisking other ingredients. This creates an emulsion
- Once pork chops are cooked, pour vinaigrette over them and serve

Ketogenic Soup and Salad Recipes

The variety of soup and salad recipes packed into this chapter are for sure great with any meal you choose to make from previous chapters! They are great paired with entrees or fantastic consumed by themselves!

Soups

Thai Coconut Chicken Soup

325 Calories
20 grams of Fat
29 grams of Protein
7 grams of Net Carbs

Makes 4 servings

What's in it:

- 1 ½ c. coconut cream
- 10 ounces of mixed mushrooms
- 1 pound of boneless, skinless chicken thighs
- ½ tsp. sea salt
- 1 pinch of freshly grated ginger
- 10 kaffir lime leaves or 1 lime

- 2 stalks of lemongrass
- 6 c. chicken broth
- *Optional: 1 tbsp. fish sauce*
- *Optional: 1 chili pepper*
- Cilantro (for taste and garnish)

How it's made:

- In a soup pot, heat up broth over medium-high heat
- With blunt end of a knife, whack lemongrass stalks to release the aroma. Proceed to cut into 4 1" pieces
- Add lemongrass to chicken broth along with sea salt, ginger, and lime leaves
- Let broth simmer for around 20 minutes, then strain out the solid elements
- Add chicken thighs into strained broth along with mushrooms. Let cook for 20 minutes
- Take out thighs and shred them. Add them back to broth along with coconut cream (and fish sauce if desired)
- Cook for another 5 minutes. Taste and season with more salt if desired
- Split among 4 bowls to serve and top with chili pepper and cilantro or parsley

Keto Fat Bomb Hamburger Soup

What's in it:

- ¼ c. freshly chopped parsley
- A pinch of cayenne pepper
- ½ tsp. chili powder
- 1 bay leaf
- 1 tbsp. tomato paste
- 2 c. whole tomatoes
- 4 c. homemade beef stock, with the fat
- 6 sticks of celery
- 3 minced cloves of garlic
- 1 pound of grass-fed ground beef
- Freshly ground pepper, to taste
- Himalayan rock salt, to taste
- ¼ c. melted red palm oil
- 20 halved Brussels sprouts
- 1 sliced yellow bell pepper
- 10 chopped mushrooms
- ½ sliced red onion

How it's made:

- Ensure oven is preheated to 350 degrees
- On a large baking sheet, spread out palm oil, Brussels sprouts, bell pepper, mushrooms and onions and then season nicely with salt and pepper
- Stick in the oven to allow to roast for 25-30 minutes. When done, set to the side

- In a large soup pot, pour in ground beef and cook over medium-low heat until everything is adequately cooked through. Add in celery and garlic and cook for an additional 3 minutes. ***Do not drain any fat***
- Pour in the remainder of the ingredients and bring to a boil
- Lessen your heat to low and simmer for 15-20 minutes
- Add in newly roasted veggies and parsley
- Enjoy!

5 Minute Cream of Tomato Soup

187 Calories
15.9 grams of Fat
3.5 grams of Protein
7.7 grams of Net Carbs

What's in it:

- 4 c. hot water
- 1 clove of garlic
- ¼ tsp. black pepper
- ½ tsp. white pepper
- ¼ c. fresh basil
- 1 tsp. sea salt
- ½ c. raw macadamia nuts
- ½ c. sun dried tomatoes
- 4 Roma tomatoes

How it's made:

- In a high-powered blender, add in all ingredients and blend on high for 5 minutes until heated through
- Serve and enjoy!

Cream of Broccoli Soup

123 Calories
Fat – 3.9 grams
Protein – 6.9 grams
Net Carbs – 11.5 grams

What's in it:

- 1 tbsp. onion powder
- 3 c. finely chopped broccoli florets
- 3 c. unsweetened almond milk
- 4 c. cauliflower florets
- Freshly ground pepper, to taste
- 1 tsp. sea salt
- 1 sliced yellow onion
- 1 tsp. extra-virgin olive oil

How it's made:

- Add salt, pepper, onion and oil in a saucepan. Sauté over medium-high heat for 5 minutes, adding a bit of water here and there if needed to avoid unnecessary burning
- Pour in milk and cauliflower. Cover pan and then proceed to bring to a boil.

Lessen your heat and simmer covered for about 10 minutes or until florets are soft with the touch of a fork

- Pour mixture into a blender high in power and blend and/or puree until mixture is smooth in texture
- Return mixture back to its pot
- Pour and mix in remaining broccoli and onion powder. Cook covered for an additional 10 minutes, until nice and thick
- Serve right away

Pump Up Your Greens 'Creamed' Soup

95 Calories
7.6 grams of Fat
2.1 grams of Protein
2.5 grams of Net Carbs

What's in it:

- Freshly ground pepper, to taste
- Pinch of chili powder
- 1 tbsp. lemon juice
- 1 tbsp. soy seasoning
- 1 clove of garlic
- ¼ c. gluten-free vegetable broth
- ½ c. red bell pepper
- 1 green onion
- ½ c. cucumber
- 1 avocado
- 2 c. spinach leaves

How it's made:

- In a blender, pop in all ingredients and blend and/or puree until the mixture is nice and smooth in texture
- Serve!

Grain-Free Cream of Mushroom Soup

95 Calories
4 grams of Fat
4.9 grams of Protein
7.9 grams of Net Carbs

What's in it:

- ½ diced yellow onion
- 1 ½ c. diced white mushrooms
- ½ tsp. olive oil
- Freshly ground pepper
- ¼ tsp. Himalayan rock salt
- 1 tsp. onion powder
- 1 2/3 c. unsweetened original almond milk
- 2 c. cauliflower florets

How it's made:

- In small saucepan, pour in salt, pepper, onion powder, milk, and cauliflower. Cover pan over medium heat and bring it to a boil

- Lessen your heat and simmer for 7-8 minutes until the cauliflower is soft enough to stick with a fork or toothpick
- In a food processor, puree cauliflower mixture
- Meanwhile, in a saucepan, add onion, mushrooms, and oil over high heat, cooking until onions are translucent in color. This takes 8 minutes
- Add in your pureed cauliflower mixture to sautéed mushrooms. Bring everything to a boil and then proceed in simmering for 10 minutes or at least until mixture is nice and thick
- Serve!

Roasted Garlic Soup

73 Calories
2.4 grams of Fat
2.1 grams of Protein
9.2 grams of Net Carbs

What's in it:

- Freshly ground pepper
- ¾ tsp. sea salt
- 6 c. vegetable broth, preferably gluten-free
- 5 c. chopped cauliflower (1 large head)
- 3 chopped shallots
- 1 tbsp. extra-virgin olive oil
- 2 bulbs of garlic

How it's made:

- Ensure oven is preheated to 400 degrees
- Peel skin off of garlic as much as you possibly can while also keeping individual bulbs together. Cut ¼" from the top of the bulb and place it within a square piece of foil. Coat each piece of the bulb with oil and place in oven for 35 minutes
- Allow garlic to cool awhile before removing foil and proceeding to squeeze juices out of each clove of garlic
- In a medium saucepan, pour remaining olive oil and bring up the heat to medium-high. Mix in shallots, sautéing them until they are tender and start to brown
- Pour in your now roasted garlic and the remainder of ingredients. Cover pan and then bring contents up to a boil. Then lessen your heat to low and simmer for 15-20 minutes until cauliflower is soft in texture
- In a blender, puree cauliflower and garlic mixture until it is silky in texture. Season with a hefty amount of salt and pepper to taste if desired and serve

Crock-Pot Chicken and Rutabaga Greens Stew

194 Calories
2.9 grams of Fat

22.8 grams of Protein
14.5 grams of Net Carbs

What's in it:

- ¼ tsp. freshly ground pepper
- ¼ tsp. chili powder
- ¼ tsp. turmeric
- ½ tsp. sea salt
- ½ tsp. oregano
- ½ tsp. mustard seeds
- 1 tsp. kelp flakes
- 2 tsp. ground cumin
- 1 chicken bouillon cube dissolved in 2 cups water
- 2 minced cloves of garlic
- 1 chopped orange pepper
- 1 peeled and slice yellow onion
- 1 bunch of chopped kale (2 cups)
- 2 large carrots, cut into ¼" discs
- 2 c. rutabaga, cut into 1" pieces
- 4 skinless, boneless chicken breasts

How it's made:

- In the bottom of a slow cooker, mix together chicken, rutabaga, carrots, kale, yellow onion, orange pepper, and garlic until combined
- In a large bowl, mix together remaining ingredients. Pour over top of chicken

mixture that already is sitting in the slow cooker

- Do NOT stir. Cover slow cooker and set cooker to cook on low for 9-10 hours or on high for 4-5 hours
- Serve with a nice big pinch of kelp flakes on top for a good dose of delicious color

Where It Vegan Gazpacho

147 Calories
9 grams of Fat
2.9 grams of Protein
13.4 grams of Net Carbs

What's in it:

- 1 batch of croutons
- Salt and pepper, to taste
- 1/8 tsp. white powdered stevia
- ¼ c. finely chopped parsley
- ¼ c. white wine vinegar
- ¼ c. olive oil
- 3 ½ c. tomato juice
- 1 crushed clove of garlic
- 6 finely chopped stalks of celery
- ½ green pepper, finely chopped and seeded
- ½ cucumber, finely chopped
- 1 finely chopped red onion

How it's made:

- In a food processor, pour in the first 6 ingredients and pulse with an 'S' blade until all ingredients are broken up
- Place all ingredients in a bowl and combine. Chill at the very least 3 hours. The more the better!
- Serve with croutons

Salads

Dr. Mercola's Keto Salad

What's in it:

- 10-20 shakes of ground pepper
- 4-7 shakes of Himalayan salt
- 3 ounces of fermented veggies
- 2-3 ounces of grass-fed pastured butter
- 1 tbsp. salmon fish roe
- 1 chopped habanero pepper
- 1 handful of Malabar spinach
- 100 grams of red pepper
- 2 finely chopped sprigs of rosemary
- 2-4 ounces of fennel leaves
- 1 handful of finely cut oregano
- 6 pieces of anchovies
- 1-2 tbsp. extra-virgin coconut oil
- 2-4 ounces of sunflower seed sprouts
- 1 avocado
- 1/3 red onion
- 2 ounces of ground lamb

How it's made:

- In a frying pan, gently heat up the extra-virgin coconut oil
- Add ground lamb and onions to oil on low heat and heat for 20-25 minutes
- Cut and mix up the remaining ingredients in a separate bowl
- After 25 minutes is up, pour in onions to salad and mix up well
- Rinse anchovies and soak for about 5 minutes
- Split anchovies and add to salad
- Add lamb to salad and enjoy!

Cobb Salad

670 Calories
Fat – 48 grams
Protein – 50 grams
Net Carbs – 5 grams

Makes 1 serving

What's in it:

- Salt and pepper
- 1 tbsp. apple cider vinegar
- 1 tbsp. olive oil
- 1 head of romaine lettuce
- 1 large hard boiled egg
- 1 ounce of cheddar cheese
- 3 ½ ounces of chicken breast

- ½ of a medium avocado
- 1 slice of bacon

How it's made:

- Chop up lettuce and dump in a salad bowl
- Chop up all the other ingredients and place them in piles on top of bed of lettuce
- Salt and pepper to your liking, add oil and vinegar and your choice of dressing and enjoy!

<u>Mixed Green Spring Salad</u>

478 Calories
37.3 grams of Fat
17.1 grams of Protein
4.3 grams of Net Carbs

What's in it:

- Salt and pepper, to taste
- 2 slices of bacon
- 2 tbsp. of shaved parmesan
- 2 tbsp. of *5 Minute Keto Raspberry Vinaigrette* (recipe later in chapter)
- 3 tbsp. roasted pine nuts
- 2 ounces of mixed greens

How it's made:

- Cook up bacon until it is crisp. It is even better if the edges are slightly burnt
- Measure out greens and put in a container that has room to shake ingredients in
- Crumble up bacon and add rest of ingredients to greens. Shake the container to distribute the dressing and contents
- Serve!

Thai Shrimp Salad

Makes 2 servings

What's in it:

- Pinch of course salt
- Pinch of freshly ground pepper
- Cilantro
- Mint leaves
- Crushed peanuts
- ½ c. thinly sliced sweet peppers
- ½ c. halved cherry tomatoes
- 4 c. shredded romaine lettuce
- 2 bundles of vermicelli noodles (previously boiled and rinsed in a cold bath)
- 1 c. blanched and cooled sugar snap peas

- ½ pound of peeled and deveined shrimp
- 1 tbsp. minced red pepper
- 3 tbsp. lime juice
- 1 tbsp. brown sugar
- 1 tsp. sambal oelek
- 1 tsp. fish sauce
- 2 tbsp. soy sauce
- 6 tbsp. olive oil (divided)

How it's made:

- Whisk together 4 tbsp. of oil, then soy sauce, fish sauce, sambal oelek, sugar, lime juice and minced red pepper in a medium sized bowl
- Over medium-high heat, heat up remaining oil in a skillet. Pour in shrimp, ensuring that you season adequately with salt and pepper
- Sear shrimp on both sides for 1-2 minutes
- Get out 2 salad bowls and start building your salad. Put some romaine lettuce to start, add your noodles, snow peas, peppers, shrimp, tomatoes, cilantro, mint, and peanuts
- Mix up dressing before applying to salad
- Enjoy!

Prosciutto, Melon and Spinach Salad

Makes 2 servings

What's in it:

- ¼ c. diced red onion
- Handful of unsalted, raw walnuts
- 1 avocado
- 1 cantaloupe
- 1/3 pound of prosciutto
- 2 c. baby spinach

How it's made:

- Get out two plates and place a cup of baby spinach on each plate
- Top spinach with walnuts, red onion, slices of avocado, balls of melon and diced up prosciutto
- Season with freshly ground pepper, to taste
- Serve with favorite dressing

Sirloin Steak Salad with Gorgonzola and Pine Nuts

Makes 4 servings

What's in it:

- 6 ounces of crumbled Gorgonzola cheese

- 3 tbsp. toasted pine nuts
- 8 c. mixed baby greens
- 1 minced clove of garlic
- 2 tsp. Dijon mustard
- 1 tbsp. red wine vinegar
- 2 tsp. minced fresh rosemary
- Salt and pepper, to taste
- 5 tbsp. olive oil
- 2 – 1 pound sirloin steaks

How it's made:

- Rub each side of steak with oil and ensure to season generously with salt and pepper
- Rub rosemary on each side of steak. Let stand at room temperature for about 1 hour. Or, chill uncovered for 4 hours and remove 40 minutes before cooking
- Over medium-high heat, heat up a cast-iron skillet. Put steaks in pan and cook each side 2-3 minutes each. Cook to your liking until meat is 120-125 degrees (for rare) Transfer meat to a platter to let sit
- Mix together vinegar, mustard, garlic, ½ tsp. salt and lots of pepper in a small to medium sized bowl. Whisk well to combine. Add remaining olive oil to the mixture. Whisk until emulsified
- Put your greens in a serving bowl and arrange them. Cut steak across the grain into slices around ½" thick and

put on salad. Top with pine nuts and Gorgonzola cheese and drizzle with dressing

Salad Dressings

5 Minute Keto Raspberry Vinaigrette

What's in it:

- ½ c. golden raspberries
- 35 drops of liquid stevia
- ½ c. extra virgin olive oil
- ½ c. white wine vinegar

How it's made:

- In an immersion blender, combine liquid stevia, olive oil, and vinegar.
- Add raspberries and blend with immersion blender
- Strain the seeds from the vinaigrette. Discard seeds
- Enjoy with your favorite salads!

Fat Burning Salad Dressings

21.3 grams of Fat
0.4 grams of Protein
0.8 grams of Net Carbs

Makes 6 servings

What's in it:

- 2 tbsp. freshly chopped herbs of choice
- 2 tbsp. fresh lemon juice
- 2 cloves of garlic
- 2 tbsp. MCT oil
- ¼ c. extra virgin olive oil
- 1 tbsp. Dijon mustard
- ¼ c. mayo

Optional Ingredients

- 1 tbsp. ketchup
- 1 tbsp. Sriracha
- ¼ tsp. chili powder
- ½ tbsp. garlic powder

How it's made:

- Peel and crush garlic. In a jar, add MCT oil, olive oil, mustard, garlic, lemon juice, and mayo. Season with salt and pepper to taste. Pour in your chopped herbs
- Put the lid on a jar and shake until everything is well combined. Chill for up to a week
- *Make sure to shake up dressing before topping salads with it*

Dairy-Free Ranch Dressing

What's in it:

- 1 tbsp. finely diced fresh parsley
- 1 tbsp. dried chives
- ¼ tsp. celery seed
- 1 clove of garlic
- 1 tsp. Dijon mustard
- 1 tsp. coconut aminos
- 2 tsp. dehydrated onion
- 1 tbsp. chia seeds
- ¼ c. lemon juice
- ¼ c. unsalted and raw sunflower seeds
- 1 c. non-dairy milk

How it's made:

- Add all ingredients but the chives and parsley in a high-powered blender and blend for 2 minutes or until smooth
- Transfer dressing to a resealable jar, then stir in parsley and chives. Chill overnight

Ketogenic Dessert Recipes

<u>Keto Lava Cake</u>

173 Calories
13 grams of Fat
8 grams of Protein
4 grams of Net Carbs

Makes 1 serving

What's in it:

- 1 pinch of salt
- ¼ tsp. baking powder
- ½ tsp. vanilla extract
- 1 tbsp. heavy cream
- 1 medium egg
- 1-2 tbsp. erythritol
- 2 tbsp. cocoa powder

How it's made:

- Ensure oven is preheated to 350 degrees
- In a small bowl, mix together cocoa powder and erythritol until there are no more clumps
- Beat egg until it is of a fluffy consistency in another bowl. Add egg, vanilla

extract and heavy cream to the sugar and cocoa mixture. Add salt and baking powder in too

- Spray mugs or ramekins with cooking spray and pour batter in. Bake for 10-15 minutes. Top of cake should be jiggly in texture
- Let cool before consuming. Enjoy with a scoop of ice cream if desired

1 Carb Chocolate Glazed Meringues

25 Calories
1.7 grams of Fat
1.7 grams of Protein
1 gram of Net Carbs

Makes 20-22 servings

What's in it:

- 1 pinch of salt
- 1 ½ ounces of 90% cocoa dark chocolate
- 1 tsp. vanilla extract
- 2 tbsp. unsweetened shredded coconut
- 1/16 tsp. liquid stevia
- 4 large separated eggs

How it's made:

- Ensure oven is preheated to 225 degrees

- In a bowl, beat egg whites with an electric hand mixer until soft peaks appear
- Add pinch of salt and sweetener and beat until stiff, white and shiny peaks form
- Pour in shredded coconut and vanilla extract. Fold these ingredients in gently
- Add meringue batter to a piping bag fitted with the tip of your choosing
- Cover a baking sheet with parchment paper and pipe meringues into about 3" rounds
- Bake for 50-60 minutes
- Once baked, turn off oven and leave the door ajar. Let meringues sit in the heat of the oven for 15-20 minutes to cool. This will prevent cracking
- Melt dark chocolate in a double broiler or in the microwave. Let chocolate cool for 10 minutes. Then pour on top of meringues. (You can either drizzle chocolate over them or dip them into melted chocolate.)

Low Carb Affogato (Coffee and Ice Cream Dessert)

241 Calories
Fat – 21 grams
Protein – 4 grams
Net Carbs – 2 grams

Makes 4 servings

What's in it:

Ice Cream

- 1/8 c. MCT oil
- 1 tsp. vanilla bean seeds
- ½ c. heavy cream
- 1/8 tsp. cream of tartar
- ¼ c. stevia
- 2 large eggs

Amaretto

- ¼ tsp. almond essence
- ¼ tsp. vanilla bean seeds
- 1 tsp. stevia
- 30 ml vodka
- 4 tsp. water

Coffee

- 80 ml hot water
- 32 grams of ground coffee

How it's made:

Ice Cream

- Separate your eggs and pour whites into a whisking bowl. Beat with electric mixer until eggs are white and form thick peaks. Gradually add in sweetener while mixing until egg whites no longer have a gritty feel to them

- Pour in cream of tartar and mix for another minute. This should make an even stiffer texture
- Whisk cream until it becomes thick in a separate bowl. DO NOT OVERMIX.
- In another bowl, beat egg yolks with a fork and add in vanilla bean seeds. Add MCT oil and fold into the whipped cream
- Gently fold whipped cream, eggs yolks, and vanilla seed mixture into the egg whites. You should have a light, fluffy texture. Transfer to a container lined in parchment and chill for 4 or more hours

Amaretto

- Mix all amaretto ingredients together until stevia dissolves. Pour into a container and chill for at least 3 hours

Affogato

- Makes a double shot expresso with a strong, rich bean roast. Dark roasts work the best with this recipe

- Take 1 ½ scoops of ice cream and place in a glass. Pour Amaretto over ice cream. Pour hot coffee over ice cream and liquor

Carmel Nut Clusters

90 Calories
8 grams of Fat
1 gram of Protein
1.5 grams of Net Carbs

Makes 9 servings

What's in it:

Base

- 1 tsp. coarse sea salt
- 9 sugar-free caramel candies
- 20 macadamias
- 9 pecans

Chocolate Ganache

- ¼ tsp. vanilla extract
- 40 grams of 85% dark chocolate
- 2-3 tbsp. heavy cream

How it's made:

- Ensure oven is preheated to 320 degrees
- With parchment paper or foil line a baking sheet
- Place pecans evenly on sheet and add macadamia nuts near them, making them overlap slightly

- Place a caramel candy onto each pile of nuts and put a sheet into the oven.
- Bake for 10 minutes until caramels are touching all the nuts. Do not allow caramels to melt into large puddles
- While caramels are cooling, heat heavy cream in a double broiler until is just starts to bubble. Drop dark chocolate into cream, and stir gently
- Once chocolate is silky and smooth, add 1/2 – 1 tsp. onto each pile of nuts.
- Sprinkle some sea salt on top while chocolate is still wet
- Chill for about an hour and then feel free to enjoy!

Low Carb Peanut Butter Cookies

105 Calories
Fat – 9 grams
Protein – 4 grams
Net Carbs – 2 grams

Makes 15 servings

What's in it:

- 1 egg
- ½ c. erythritol
- 1 c. peanut butter

How it's made:

- Ensure oven is preheated to 350 degrees
- Combine egg, erythritol and peanut butter until well mixed together in a bowl
- Roll cookie dough into 1" sized balls and place on a parchment paper lined baking sheet
- Press down on cookie balls with a fork twice to create that peanut butter cookie pattern everyone enjoys
- Bake for 10-15 minutes or until the edges of cookies are dark brown in terms of color
- Give cookies time to cool on a wire rack before serving. Enjoy!

Coconut Chocolate Bars

210 Calories
Fat – 22 grams
Protein – 1 gram
Net Carbs – 4.8 grams

What's in it:

- 2 ounces of cocoa butter
- 2 tbsp. unsweetened cocoa powder
- 4 tbsp. coconut oil
- 1/3 c. coconut cream
- 1 tsp. vanilla extract

- ½ tsp. stevia
- 1 c. shredded and unsweetened coconut

How it's made:

- In a bowl, pour in shredded coconut, coconut cream, half of the stevia and half of the vanilla and combine well
- On a cookie sheet lined with parchment paper, place shredded coconut mixture upon it
- Shape coconut mixture into a nice and flat rectangle that measures to be about 4x6" and 1" in thickness
- Put in freezer to chill for 2 hours or until nice and frozen
- Remove from chilling and cut into 5 bars
- To make chocolate coating, melt your coconut oil in a saucepan until it is liquid
- Then add remaining stevia and cocoa powder along with remaining vanilla extract to the oil
- Mix for 2 minutes over low heat until everything is well mixed
- Let cool but ensure that it stays in a liquid form
- Dip your coconut bars in the chocolate mixture and ensure you coat all sides evenly
- When you have coated all bars, put tray in the fridge to that they can harden
- Yum!

Keto Mocha Mousse

What's in it:

Cream Cheese Mixture

- 3 tsp. instant coffee powder
- ¼ c. unsweetened cocoa powder
- 1/3 c. granulated stevia
- 1 ½ tsp. vanilla extract
- 2 tbsp. softened butter
- 3 tbsp. sour cream
- 8 oz. softened cream cheese

Whipped Cream Mixture

- ½ tsp. vanilla extract
- 1 ½ tsp. granulated stevia
- 2/3 c. heavy whipping cream

How it's made:

- With an electric hand mixer, beat butter, sour cream, and cream cheese until smooth in texture
- Mix in coffee powder, cocoa powder, sweetener and vanilla extract into cream cheese mixture until well combined and set to the side
- Beat whipping cream until nice and soft peaks form in a separate bowl

- Proceed by pouring in sweetener and vanilla, continuing to beat until peaks form
- Fold the whipped cream mixture into the cream cheese mixture. Ensure that you are not deflating bubbles that will appear. Fold in the rest of mixture until whipped cream is incorporated thoroughly
- Pour your delicious mousse into dishes of your choice and then chill for 2 ½ hours until they are set and ready to enjoy!

<u>Mocha Cheesecake Bars</u>

What's in it:

Brownie Layer

- 1 tsp. baking powder
- 1 c. erythritol
- ½ tsp. salt
- ½ c. baking cocoa
- ½ tbsp. instant coffee
- 1 ½ c. almond flour
- 3 eggs
- 2 tsp. vanilla extract
- 6 tbsp. unsalted butter

Cream Cheese Layer

- 1 egg
- 1 tsp. vanilla extract

- ½ c. erythritol
- 1 pound of softened cream cheese

How it's made:

- Ensure that your oven is preheated to 350 degrees
- Prepare an 8x8 baking pan with spray
- Mix up 2 teaspoons vanilla and unsalted butter in a large bowl until well combined. Then add and mix in the 3 eggs.
- In a separate bowl, combine baking powder, salt, sweetener, baking cocoa, instant coffee and almond flour. Then proceed to pour in wet ingredients.
- Set aside at least ¼ of a cup of batter for later
- Add the bigger portion of batter into the greased pan
- Using an electric hand mixer, blend cream cheese, vanilla, sweetener and egg in a mixing bowl until nice and smooth. Spread cream cheese mixture over the brownie layer in baking pan
- Now take the reserved brownie batter and mix it into the cream cheese layer to create a type of crust. This layer should be thin
- Bake for 30-35 minutes
- Let brownies completely cool before you cut into slices

Keto Vanilla Bean Cupcakes
What's in it:

Batter

- 2 tsp. baking powder
- ¼ tsp. salt
- ½ c. erythritol
- 1 ¾ c. almond flour
- 1 tbsp. vanilla bean paste
- ½ c. mayo
- 2 eggs

Vanilla Cream Cheese Frosting

- ½ tsp. vanilla extract
- 3 tbsp. heavy whipping cream
- ¼ c. erythritol, powdered finely in a grinder
- 4 oz. softened cream cheese

How it's made:

- Ensure your oven is preheated to 350 degrees
- In a bowl, combine vanilla bean paste, mayo and eggs until very smooth. You may need a hand mixer to assist you with this. Then set this bowl to the side
- Combine baking powder, salt, sweetener and almond flour in a large bowl

- Gradually whisk in the wet ingredients into the dry ingredients. Recommended to utilize a hand mixer for this step
- The mixture will appear dry, this is what you want
- Into a cupcake pan filled with liners, use a ¼ cup measurer to spoon out eight servings
- Bake for 20-25 minutes until cupcakes appear lightly browned.
- Allow cakes to cool and then frost them

Conclusion

Thanks for making it through to the end of *Ketogenic Diet for Beginners*. I hope the contents of this book were able to provide you with adequate information to get you started on the right path to a healthier, better version of yourself!

I hope that what you have absorbed has provided you with just the right information for you to make the decision to create and build a body that you will be proud to show off! I hope that it gave you the tools you will need to achieve your health and/or weight loss goals.

The next step is to get off that couch, throw away that bag of potato chips and get to work! Even though you have just read some pretty great information that could lead you to create an entirely new you (on the outside, that is), that does not mean that something is going to happen without you following the guidelines of the ketogenic diet and really becoming motivated into helping yourself feel more alive. Isn't it about time you stopped the excuses and actually did something for yourself and your health?

I wish you much luck as you conquer the delicious recipes shared with you within this book and that you will spread the amazing results you will find from the ketogenic diet with loved ones. You have nothing to lose!

Finally, if you found this book useful in any way, a review on Amazon is always appreciated!

Made in the USA
San Bernardino, CA
15 January 2018